IMAGES
of Sport

DUNDEE FOOTBALL CLUB
1893-1977

Dundee FC postcard *c*. 1900.

IMAGES
of Sport

DUNDEE FOOTBALL CLUB
1893-1977

Compiled by
Paul Lunney

TEMPUS

Tempus Publishing Limited
The Mill, Brimscombe Port,
Stroud, Gloucestershire, GL5 2QG

ISBN 0 7524 2230 8

Typesetting and origination by
Tempus Publishing Limited
Printed in Great Britain by
Midway Colour Print, Wiltshire

Gordon Wallace shoots past the outstretched arms of Celtic 'keeper Ally Hunter to score the only goal of the 1973/74 League Cup final at Hampden Park.

Contents

Centre half Bill 'Plum' Longair with the medals, trophies and mementos he won and collected during his playing career.

Introduction

Our Boys and East End amalgamated to form Dundee Football Club in May 1893, and the new outfit's application for membership of the Scottish League was accepted at that organisation's AGM the following month. The Dark Blues gained a reputation for being a good footballing side from the very start and possessed the perfect pivot in 'Plum' Longair. However, it wasn't until their tenth term in office that they seriously contested for Scotland's top honours in the association game. Dundee came close to pulling off a remarkable league and Cup double in 1902/03, but in the end finished runners-up to Hibs in the league title race and also lost out to Edinburgh opposition at the semi-final stage of the Scottish Cup by going down 1-0 to Hearts after a replay. This was the first great Dundee team and included legendary figures such as the internationalists Billy Muir, Peter Robertson and Sandy McFarlane. Having missed out by a single point to Celtic in the 1908/09 Division One Championship, Dundee made amends the following season by capturing the Scottish Cup after a hard fought campaign which included ten ties, five replays and a second replayed final against Clyde before they eventually took the Blue Riband prize 2-1 at Ibrox on 20 April 1910. The men who achieved this Scottish Cup success for the first and, so far, only time were as follows: Crumley, Neal, McEwan, Lee, Dainty, Cromrie, Bellamy, Langlands, Hunter, McFarlane and Fraser. The result was never in doubt considering they were managed by 'braveheart' himself, one William Wallace.

Dundee's next tilt at the trophy came in 1925 when they faced Celtic in the final at Hampden. Although the Dark Blues led for a long time through a Dave McLean goal, two late strikes by Patsy Gallacher and Jimmy McGrory stole the silver from Dundee's grasp. Thankfully, the immediate post-war years would provide better luck on the domestic front. A 'B' Division Championship title triumph in 1946/47 was almost eclipsed in 1948/49 with a Scottish League 'A' Division flag, but unfortunately a dreadful 1-4 deficit at Falkirk put paid to that dream. A 'Flash of Steel' arrived at Dens Park in 1950 for a Scots record transfer fee of £17,500, and silver success was soon to follow in the form of back-to-back League Cup final victories in 1951/52 and 1952/53. Under the manager Bob Shankly the waiting was over, and in 1962 up went the bonnets with the winning of the ultimate honour which had proved so elusive. Dundee's Dark Blues were at last the top team in the country – Champions of Scotland The eleven which took the title and remained almost unchanged throughout the campaign were: Liney; Hamilton, Cox; Seith, Ure, Wishart; Smith, Penman, Cousin, Gilzean and Robertson. It rolls off the tongue sweetly and reads like a much-loved litany to every Dark Blues fan.

European Cup football beckoned in 1962/63, and only the eventual winners A.C.Milan defeated Dundee at the penultimate stage of the competition. 1967/68 was a good season for the club and only narrow reverses in the League Cup final against Celtic, and at Leeds in the Fairs Cup semi-final, deprived Dens of any silverware. The 1970s saw the Dark Blues lose an incredible five Scottish Cup semi-finals to Celtic, nonetheless each and every clash was a tight affair. Jewels in Dundee's crown during this period were that terrific inside forward trio of Gordon Wallace, John Duncan and Jocky Scott, and it was through a beautifully-executed shot from Wallace that Dundee triumphed in the 1973/74 League Cup final over Celtic.

This volume is a pictorial account of Dundee's first eighty-four years and is a tribute to star players and major triumphs of yesteryear.

'Such stuff as memories are made of.'

Paul Lunney
May 2001

Acknowledgements

I would like to thank the following for their assistance in making this book possible: Stuart Marshall of Collectors World, Derek Taylor and Raymond Taylor from Kollectables in Glasgow, *The Sunday Mail, The Scottish Daily Express*, D.C. Thomson, Jack Murray, David Crotty, Bob Holmes and everyone at Tempus Publishing, especially James Howarth.

One

The Early Years and Scottish Cup Glory
(1893-1919)

Beefy back Barney Battles joined Dundee in 1897, due to a fall out with Celtic's directors. In November 1896, Battles, Divers and Meehan refused to strip for an important clash against Hibs unless certain newspaper critics were removed from the press box. Celtic took a high moral line and offloaded all three players before the season's end. Glasgow-born Barney had offers to go to England but had given his word to Dundee. A brave figure in the Dark Blue jersey, he broke his wrist on 28 January 1898 and played the following two matches (in which Dundee knocked Hearts out of the Cup 3-0 and also defeated Rangers 2-1, with Barney scoring!) with his arm in splints and held in a sling. Barney Battles represented Scotland and the Scottish League, and died suddenly at the age of thirty on 9 November 1905 of pneumonia. At his funeral there was an enormous cortège of 2,000 people while another 40,000 lined the route to Dalbeth cemetery. His son, also called Barney, starred at centre forward for Hearts and Scotland.

VICTORY BLEND

Bob Blyth

Dundee 1895-97

FIX '59

'Jolly Jack's Mixture'
OPEN SERIES

Caricature of former Portsmouth and Preston North End half-back Bob Blyth who made 9 league appearances for Dundee in 1897/98 season and scored twice.

Dundee 1895/96. From left to right, back row: Mr J. McIntosh, Mr T. Shaw, Mr W.T. Kennedy, Johnny Darroch, Fred Barrett, Charlie Burgess, Mr W. Saunders, Mr J. Black (referee), -?-.. Front row: Mr J. McMahon, Willie Thomson, Sandy Gilligan, Bill Hendry, Bill Longair, George Phillip, Alex Black, Sandy Keillor, Adam Marshall (trainer).

The Dundee and St Bernard's players and officials before the opening match at Dens Park on 19 August 1899.

William Wallace – what a great name for a Scotsman. He was the club secretary and became Dundee's first manager in 1899 on a part-time basis. He resigned in 1919 after twenty years' sterling service to the Dark Blues' cause.

Local lad Fred McDiarmid was awarded a medal for scoring Dundee's first goal at Dens Park (against St Bernard's) in 1899. A flying outside left at the turn of the century, he formed a deadly wing partnership with Tommy McDermott before the latter joined Celtic in October 1901.

An action shot of Dens Park in the early 1900s. The postcard was sent by Johnny Darroch who has marked his presence with a cross.

Action from a Dundee *v*. Rangers clash at Dens Park in the early 1900s.

Dundee team group photo taken before the above game with Rangers at Dens Park.

Cartoon of Dundee's 1-0 Scottish Cup third round, second replay win over Hibernian at Ibrox in 1903.

Portrait of goalkeeping great Billy Muir. Born in Ayr on 22 September 1877, he played for Glenbuck Cherrypickers, Third Lanark and Kilmarnock before moving south to Everton for £45 in April 1897. Muir joined the Dark Blues in the summer of 1902 and gave them consistently steady performances for five seasons. A Scottish Junior, League and full internationalist, he subsequently starred at Bradford, Hearts and Dumbarton.

Billy Muir's one and only full international cap for Scotland against Ireland at Parkhead on 16 March 1907. He kept a clean sheet as the Scots won 3-0.

Left: Muir's Scottish League gold medal for the match against the Football League at Ibrox on 2 March 1907. The game ended goalless. *Right:* Muir's Dewar Shield 1903 winners' gold badge. Dundee won 2-1 at Victoria United.

'Sandy' MacFarlane, a legendary figure in the annals of Dundee FC. A sturdy inside forward, Sandy signed from Newcastle United in November 1901 and provided the Dark Blues with a decade of dedicated play. Capped for Scotland and the Scottish League, MacFarlane played in the 1910 Scottish Cup triumph and had two spells each in the managerial hot seat at Dens Park and Charlton Athletic.

Bob Holmes' drawings of Jimmy Burnett and 'Sailor' Hunter.

Dundee's club colours.

Diminutive outside right Alan Bell made exactly 100 league and Cup appearances for Dundee between 1902 and 1907 and netted 17 goals in the process.

Dundee FC 1905/06. Back row, fourth from left: Billy Muir. Fourth from right: John Darroch. Front row, middle trio: Sandy MacFarlane, Herbert Dainty, Fred McDiarmid.

Cartoon of the Dundee *v.* Rangers Scottish Cup tie at Dens Park in 1909. The game attracted a record ground attendance of 28,000 and finished goalless.

Strong centre forward John Hunter, nicknamed 'Sailor' because of his rolling gait, joined Dundee in 1907 having previously starred at Liverpool, Hearts, Arsenal and Portsmouth. He scored the winning goal in the 1910 Scottish Cup final win over Clyde and signed for that Glasgow club early in the following season. 'Sailor' served Motherwell as manager and secretary from 1911 to 1959. Born at Johnstone on 6 April 1878, he died on 12 January 1966, aged eighty-seven.

Dundee versus Celtic at Parkhead in the early 1900s – notice the old Pavilion and the cement track (which was laid for the 1897 World Cycling Championships) around the perimeter of the pitch.

Striker Alexander Hall cost Dundee £200 from Newcastle United in March 1908. Born at Peterhead, Hall won the Scottish League Division Two Championship with St Bernards in 1906/07 before going to Tyneside in April 1907.

GALLAHER'S CIGARETTES.

H. DAINTY,
DUNDEE 1909-10.

Skipper of Dundee's 1910 Scottish Cup-winning side, centre half Herbert Dainty made over 200 league and Cup appearances for Dundee. He represented the Scottish League against the Southern League on 24 October 1910, and moved to Bradford City in 1911. Dainty later became player/manager at both Ayr United and Dundee Hibs.

Dundee 1909/10. From left to right, back row: W. Wallace (secretary and manager), J. Chaplin, J. Fraser, A. Lee, B. Neal, R. Crumley, J. Dundas (linesman). Front row: J. Bellamy, G. Langlands, A. MacFarlane, H. Dainty, A. Menzies, J. Lawson, W. Longair (trainer).

The three 'Berts' – Al(bert) Lee, Her(bert) Dainty and Ro(bert) Neal. They all played in the 1910 Scottish Cup success over Clyde.

Custodian Crumley was a local lad who cost Dundee £50 from Newcastle United during the 1907 close season. Robert J. or Bob, as he was more familiarly known, gained recognition when playing with the Gordon Highlanders, with whom he won the Army Cup. Crumley began his career at Lochee United. His brother, James, kept goal for Dundee Hibs, while his son played for Darlington in the 1920s.

Dundee won the Scottish Cup in 1910 after three tough games in the final against Clyde. The first match was a 2-2 draw, the scorers being Hunter and Landlands for Dundee, Chalmers and Booth for Clyde. The first replay was a 0-0 draw. Dundee won the second replay 2-1, with Bellamy and Hunter finding the net for Dundee and Chalmers scoring for Clyde. All three matches were played at Ibrox.

Dundee with the Scottish Cup. From left to right, back row: J. Dundas (linesman), Neal, McEwan, Comrie, W. Wallace (manager), Dainty, Chaplin, Crumley, Longair (trainer). Middle row: Hall, Hunter, Langlands, Lee, Macfarlane, Lawson, Fraser. Front row: Bellamy, McCann.

Scottish League international John Fowler Chaplin arrived at Dens Park from Dundee Wanderers in 1903 and had two spells with the club. In 1905 he joined Spurs but returned in 1908 to take over his brother George's place in defence. He missed the third game of the 1910 final through injury, and moved to Manchester City in November of the same year. Subsequently trainer of Huddersfield Town under the astute managership of friend Herbert Chapman, he also managed the Yorkshire club to an FA Cup final in 1928. John Chaplin died in Doncaster in April 1952 at the age of sixty-nine.

Fringe forward Dan McCann and pivot George Philip. Hurlford lad McCann turned a 0-2 deficit against Rangers on 4 September 1909 into a 4-2 victory for Dundee, scoring two goals. A week later, Dan received the match ball beautifully done out in dark blue and white and autographed by all his team-mates. He signed for Celtic in May 1910. Skipper Philip switched to striker in 1913/14, and was transferred to Sunderland in 1914 for a Dens Park record fee of £1,500.

Reserve inside forward Fred Kemp and winger Jimmy Bellamy. Londoner Bellamy had played for Reading, Arsenal, Portsmouth and Norwich City before joining the Dark Blues in 1908. An all-time Dundee great, Bellamy later starred at Motherwell, Burnley, Fulham and Southend. He died in March 1969, aged eighty-seven.

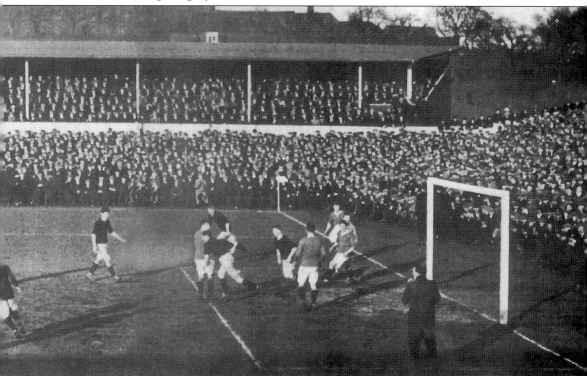

R.C. Hamilton scores for Dundee in the 2-1 win over Rangers in the Scottish Cup quarter-final tie at Dens Park on 25 February 1911.

Wonderful right-winger Billy Hogg signed for Dundee in 1913 from Rangers. A former Sunderland star forward, Billy was devil-may-care in most things, and 'gave the impression of a great big boy bubbling over with animal spirit.'

Inside forward John Barbour made 18 league and Cup appearances for Dundee in 1913/14 season and scored twice.

Two

Between The Wars
(1919-1939)

Dundee 1925/26. From left to right, back row: Vickers (trainer), Nicholson, J. Ross, Britton, Thomson, McLean. Front row: A. Ross, Irving, Brown, Rankine, Hunter, Cook.

Stylish defender David 'Napper' Thomson arrived at Dens Park in 1913 from Fairfield Juniors. His one and only cap for Scotland came in the 1-1 draw against Wales at Cardiff on 26 February 1920. 'Napper' got his nickname because of his cool collective approach. He also represented the Scottish League on two occasions.

Born in Dundee on 14 December 1896, and a product of Dundee North End, forward John Paterson made only one league appearance for the Dark Blues (a 1-0 win over Hearts on 20 September 1919) before being whisked away to Leicester City in December 1919. His form at Filbert Street was such that he received a cap against England in April 1920. Wounded five times while serving with the Black Watch during the Second World War, Paterson later starred at Sunderland and Preston North End.

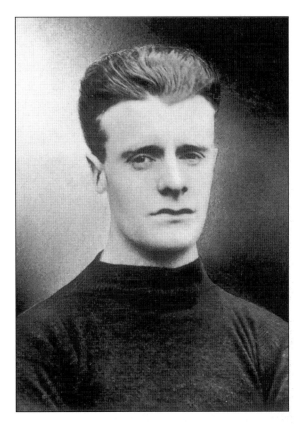

Buckhaven boy David Raitt missed only a few fixtures during his three seasons (1919 to 1922) at Dens Park in the right-back berth. A traditional tough tackler, Raitt came into prominence in Army football. He was transferred to Everton for a substantial sum in May 1922.

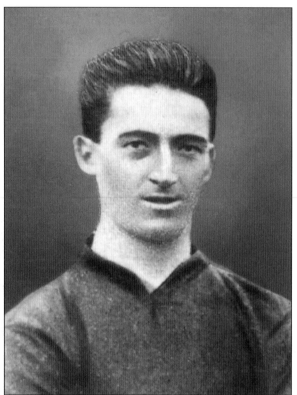

English international Archie Rawlings had one season for Dundee's Dark Blues (1919/20) before moving to Preston North End in June 1920 for £1,500. A direct and devastatingly powerful outside right, Rawlings' only cap for England came against Belgium at Brussels in May 1921. He played for many clubs including Northampton, Barnsley, Rochdale and Liverpool. He died at the age of sixty on 11 June 1952.

Centre half Dyken Nicholl signed for Dundee in 1919. A native of Forfar, he starred at centre forward with local side Celtic before going to Forfar Athletic in 1912 as a half-back. Nicholl served in the army during the First World War.

Alec Troup is an all-time Dundee great who signed from Forfar Athletic in 1915. Douglas Lamming's excellent *Who's Who of Scottish Internationalists* summed him up perfectly as a 'Diminutive wingman possessing dazzling ball control, resolution and a mastery of the measured dipping centre.' This centring ability was said to be a major contributory factor to Dixie Dean's 60 goals record in his Everton days. Alec had a weak collarbone and played every game heavily strapped. He ran a clothier's shop in his native Forfar.

Dundee FC 1919/20. From left to right, back row: Davie Raitt, David 'Napper' Thomson, Jim Watson, Dave Hutcheson, Dyken Nicholl, Bert McIntosh, Jim Downie, Jim Orr, Ernie Ferguson, Bill Longair (trainer). Front row: Archie Rawlings, Jim McLaughlan, Johnny Bell, Donald Slade, Alec Troup, Colin Buchan.

Belfast-born Samuel Johnstone Irving moved to Shildon near Newcastle as a boy. A polished performer in the wing half position, he signed for Dundee in 1920 from Blyth Spartans. In 1926 Sam went to Cardiff City and won an FA Cup winners' medal the following year. He later played at Chelsea and Bristol Rovers, and became manager of Dundee United in 1934 (and was later a director until 1958). Capped 18 times for Nothern Ireland, Sam died in Dundee on 17 January 1969, aged seventy-four.

Goalkeeper Willie Fotherington was born in Larkhall and played as a junior with Larkhall Thistle before going to Airdrieonians. He joined Dundee in 1921 and was an ever-present in 1921/22 and 1922/23. He missed a mere three starts in the 1923/24 campaign.

Dundee 1920/21. From left to right, back row: John Jackson, Dyken Nicholl, David Raitt, Tom Gibbon, Napper Thomson, George Philip, Sam Irving. Front row: Davie McDonald, Davie Bell, Donald Slade, Alec Troup.

One of football's greatest ever goalscorers, centre forward Davie McLean played for Forfar Athletic from the age of sixteen. He netted a hat-trick on his Celtic debut in 1907, but was unable to displace the legendary Jimmy Quinn and moved to Preston North End for £400 in November 1909. Capped against England in 1912 while with Sheffield Wednesday, Davie had a four-year period at Dundee, from 1922 to 1926. A superb opportunist, who was distinctive on the field because of his unusual stiff gait, McLean finished his career in 1932 with an aggregate goals total of around 500.

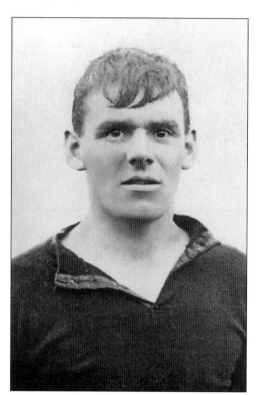

Dark Blues Maiden and Willis were two players on the fringe of a first-team place at Dens Park in the early 1920s.

Dundee forwards David Halliday and Charlie Duncan featured on the front cover of a special preview Cup final edition of the *Topical Times* in 1925.

Three comic strips of Patsy Gallacher's incredible equalizing goal against Dundee in the 1925 Scottish Cup final at Hampden Park. This was arguably the greatest goal ever scored in any of the Blue Riband finals.

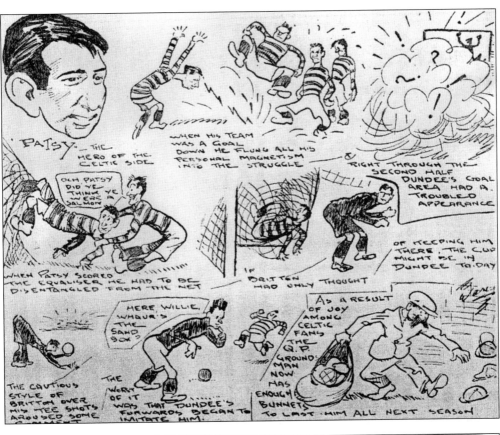

Portrait of Dundee manager Alec McNair during his playing days with Celtic. A former Scotland international and one of the finest full-backs ever to play the game, McNair held his post from 12 June 1925 until 7 October 1927. He resigned after a poor start to the 1927/28 campaign.

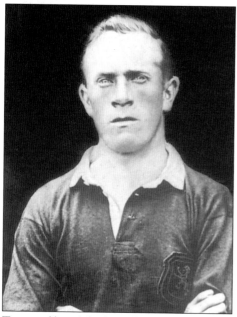

Two profiles of the legendary Alec Troup

Caricatures of Jimmy Easson and Bobby Kearny. Easson never actually played for Dundee, but did star for East Craigie from Dundee before making his name with Portsmouth and Scotland.

Willie Cook, the wee Dundonian, arrived at Dens Park in the summer of 1925 from Forfar Athletic. He was described as 'A wonderfully diverting little winger juggling the ball with panache, working chances for teammates and not averse to scoring himself.' Once a clerk with a timber firm, Cook moved to Bolton Wanderers for £3,000 in December 1928, and also had spells at Blackpool, Reading and Dundee again in 1938. He was a Scottish international and an FA Cup winner, in 1929, whilst with Bolton.

Prolific marksman Hugh Ferguson scored the famous goal for Cardiff City against Arsenal which took the FA Cup out of England for the first and only time, in 1927. He was transferred to the Welsh club on 3 November 1925 for £5,000, having scored a remarkable 362 goals for Motherwell, 283 of them in the Scottish League. When Cardiff had been relegated, Hugh joined Dundee in June 1929, and on 3 August the trial game at Dens Park drew 8,000 spectators eager for a glimpse of the thirty-four-year-old centre. Unfortunately, Dundee's high-ball tactic did not suit his style and, after a knee injury and poor form, he was dropped in December 1929. Suffering from insomnia, and in mental and physical pain on the evening of 8 January 1930, he returned to Dens Park and committed suicide.

Giant goalie Bill Marsh arrived at Dens Park in the summer of 1924 from Chelsea. At 6ft 2ins and 13st 8lbs, Marsh was a formidable figure between the posts. Born in Woodhouse, he began his career Eckington Works of Sheffield and signed for Chelsea in December 1921. A keen angler and notable golfer, Marsh moved to Kilmarnock in November 1937, and conceded 8 goals on his Killie debut on Christmas Day at Celtic Park. He made a marvellous 417 appearances for Dundee and owned a confectionary shop.

The Dundee forward line of 1931 – Gavigan, Campbell, Craigie, Robertson and Troup.

Wing-half Scot Symon attended the rugby-playing school of Perth Academy, yet became a junior soccer international before going to Dundee. A solid whole-hearted team man noted for his tackling, he was transferred to Portsmouth in 1935, and was a successful manager of East Fife, Preston North End and Rangers. The first man to represent Scotland at both football and cricket, he died on 30 April 1985.

Two-footed full-back Lew Morgan was a sound tackler who had terrific speed in recovery. A young Fifer, he came into the Dundee side during the 1931/32 season and represented the Scottish League against the Irish League at Belfast on 30 September 1933. He was sold to Pompey in August 1935, along with Scot Symon, for £7,000.

Dundee 1933/34. From left to right, back row: Johnny Murdoch, Jimmy Robertson, Bill Marsh, Tom Smith, Tom McCarthy. Front row: Harry Smith, Willie Blyth, Lou Morgan, Jock Gilmour, Danny Paterson, Pat Lee.

Irishman and Dens Park favourite Norman Kirby cost Dundee £500 from Belfast Distillery in the autumn of 1933. An outside left, Kirby was a regular choice for the Dark Blues until 1938.

Bellshill-born Jock Gilmore signed for Dundee in 1924 from Bathgate. A long-serving left-back, Jock was capped in a 1-1 draw against Wales at Ibrox on 25 October 1930. After brief spells at Yeovil & Petters United and Ross County he came out of retirement to play for Dundee United in a cup-tie in February 1938.

VICTORY BLEND

Jimmy Guthrie Dundee 1933-37

MEECH 58

'Jolly Jack's Mixture'
OPEN SERIES

A native of Luncarty, Perthshire, Jimmy
Guthrie starred for Scone Thistle and
Scotland at youth level before joining
Dundee in 1932. A creative midfield
maestro, he went on to captain the club
and also skippered Portsmouth in the 1939
FA Cup final at Wembley. In 1946 he was
appointed chairman of the Players' Union
in England.

Centre forward Archie Coats initially played for
Wishaw Juniors, Portsmouth and Bangor of
Northern Ireland. He joined Dundee in 1934 and
was an ever-present for the next three seasons. He
only missed 13 games up until 1940, when the club
closed down. A prolific scorer, Coats netted
132 goals for the Dark Blues and helped the
Scottish League defeat the Irish League 3-2 in
Belfast on 1 September 1937.

One of the Dens Park colts, centre forward Davie Reid, who signed from the local team Osborne.

Tommy Robertson was an incredibly fast outside right who signed for Dundee from Ayr United in 1934. An ex-miner from Craigview Athletic, Robertson was originally a full-back and moved on to Clyde in 1936.

Born and bred at Luncarty, Perthshire, skilful left-half Tom Smith was a childhood friend of fellow Dundee star of the 1930s, Jimmy Guthrie, and arrived at Dens Park from Perth Thistle in 1931. Smith graduated to skipper and, like Coats, won a Scottish League cap in 1937 against the Irish. He was killed in the early days of the Second World War while serving with the Fleet Air Arm.

T. SMITH

An advert for summer football. New Year's Day 1936 and Dundee's Tommy Robertson is about to take a corner at Dens Park against Aberdeen. The game ended in a 2-2 draw.

Dundee 1937/38. From left to right, back row: Adamson, Cowie, Marsh, Rennie, T. Smith, Evans. Front row: Regan, Baxter, Coats, McMenemy, Kirby.

R. RENNIE

A native of Alva. Bobby 'Tiger' Rennie was a hard-tackling red-headed full-back who signed from Clydebank Juniors in 1935. He took over Lew Morgan's job at right-back when the latter moved south to join Portsmouth.

Left: Welshman John Evans took over the centre half berth from Scot Symon in 1935 and moved on to Motherwell in 1938. *Right:* Left-back Len Richards signed from Dundalk in 1935 and made 80 League and cup appearances for Dundee.

Left: Centre forward Jimmy Balfour finished the 1931/32 season as Dundee's top league scorer, with 21 goals. *Right*: Left-half Harry Sneddon joined Dundee from Blairhall during the 1937/38 campaign.

A. COATS

Four Dark Blue favourites of the 1930s. *Above:* Lew Morgan and Archie Coats. *Below:* Scot Symon and Bill Marsh.

SYMON

Presented with Adventure

W. Marsh, Dundee.

Regarded as one of the most alert goalkeepers in Scotland in the 1940s, Johnny Lynch signed for Dundee from Cambuslang Rangers in 1935. He played much of his wartime football in the Middle East in the company of Tom Finney and Wilf Mannion, and moved to St Mirren in 1951 on a free transfer.

Dundee players relaxing in the summer of 1939. From left to right, back row: Jimmy Morgan, Coats, Masson, Arbuckle (trainer). Front row. Lynch, Kirby, Sneddon, McGillivray.

Three
Billy Steel and League Cup Successes (1939-1959)

Dundee Great Tommy Gallacher (left) poses with his father Patsy and brother Willie at Dens Park in 1948.

Dundee defenders Tommy Gray and Bobby Ancell keep tight tabs on Rangers forward Jimmy Duncanson during the 1945/46 League Cup quarter-final at Hampden Park.

BENNETT

Well known for his daring saves, custodian Reuben Bennett joined Dundee in 1944. A product of Aberdeen East End, Reuben had played for Hull City and Queen of the South before coming to Tayside. An excellent shot stopper who was also an expert at cutting out cross balls, Bennett was Dundee's trainer from 1950 to 1953 and Liverpool trainer from 1959 under Bill Shankly and Bob Paisley.

Dumfries-born Bobby Ancell was a brilliant back who had played for St Mirren and Newcastle United. He cost the Dark Blues £150 in July 1944, and he subsequently had a successful managerial career at Berwick, Dunfermline and Motherwell. He managed Dundee from 1 April 1965 until September 1968.

ANCELL

Dundee 1946/47. From left to right, back row: George Anderson, Gerry Follon, Gibby McKenzie, Reuben Bennett, Tommy Gray, Johnny Lynch, Bobby Ancell, Reggie Smith, Jack Swadel (director). Front row: Bert Juliussen, Ally Gunn, Johnny Pattillo, Ronnie Turnbull, Ernie Ewen, George Hill, Frank Joyner, Willie Cameron (trainer/masseur).

JULIUSSEN

Centre forward Albert Juliussen was signed from Huddersfield Town in July 1945 for £2,000. Born in Blyth on 20 February 1920, 'Big Julie' had served with the Black Watch during the war and was a powerful player who possessed a tremendous left-foot shot. In his first two seasons at Dens Park he hit an astounding 61 goals in 33 league games. Bert was sold to Portsmouth in March 1948 for £10,000.

VICTORY BLEND

Albert Juliussen

F1X'53   Dundee 1946-47

'Jolly Jack's Mixture'
OPEN SERIES

JULLIESON

With the game goal-less, Alec Stott's penalty is saved in the last league fixture of 1948/49 at Brockville. Falkirk eventually won 4-1 to shatter Dundee's title dream.

Dundee were league runners-up in 1948/49. From left to right, back row: George Anderson, Tommy Gallacher, Gerry Follon, Johnny Lynch, Andy Irvine, Doug Cowie, Alfie Boyd, Reggie Smith. Front row: Ally Gunn, Johnny Pattillo, Alec Stott, Syd Gerrie, George Hill.

Record crowds queue up at Dens Park for the Dundee *v*. Rangers match on 3 January 1949. The Dark Blues won 3-1 in front of an official attendance of 39,975. A few thousand more are believed to have gained entry illegally.

REGGIE SMITH

England international Reggie Smith signed from Millwall in March 1946. Although previously an outside left, he took up the left-half berth at Dens Park. After a successful period as the club's trainer, he went on to manage Dundee United, Falkirk and Millwall. His surname was actually Schmidt, and he was the son of a South African rugby international who came to Britain with the first Springboks touring side.

Son of the 'Peerless Patsy', Tommy Gallacher began his career at Queen's Park in 1942 as an inside forward, but moved back to the more influential position of right half when he arrived at Dens Park in August 1947. As a strong and forceful, yet creative, wing half, Tommy won a Scottish League cap against the Football League at Ibrox on 23 March 1949. He retired in 1956, and later became a journalist with the *Dundee Courier*.

TOMMY GALLACHER

Ally Gunn gets the better of Jock Shaw to head home against Rangers at Dens Park. Dundee won this league fixture 2-0 on 30 December 1950.

James Christopher Reginald Smith was born at Battersea, London, on 20 January 1912. He scored twice on his England debut in a 4-0 win over Norway at St James' Park on 9 November 1938, and followed that up a week later by starring in a 7-0 victory over Northern Ireland at Old Trafford. Reggie was in charge of Falkirk when they won the Scottish Cup in 1957, and subsequently managed a number of clubs in South Africa during the 1960s.

Alfie Boyd succeeded Reggie Smith at left half for Dundee in the late 1940s. A former Dens Park ball-boy, Boyd cost £4,000 from St Johnstone halfway through the 1946/47 season. He played in the 1951/52 and 1952/53 League Cup final triumphs and, like Tommy Gallacher, represented the Scottish League at Ibrox in 1949.

George 'Pud' Hill was a dashing winger who did much to bring Dundee out of the wilderness and into the forefront of Scottish football. A provisional signing in season 1939/40, he could cross the ball with great accuracy and had an amazing burst of speed. He was released in 1955 having given the club terrific service.

Centre half Tommy Gray was a splendid half-back who could also play in the full-back position. Signed from Morton in 1944, Tommy was exceptionally good with his head and an ideal stopper pivot. He moved on to Arbroath in 1949.

Wee Ernie Ewan was a tremendous hard-hitting inside forward discovered in local junior football in 1944. Strong in the tackle and very difficult to dispossess, he signed for Aberdeen in 1952 and then St Johnstone. He was a prolific scorer and a great favourite at Dens Park.

EWEN

PATTILLO

Dundee signed veteran forward Johnny Pattillo from Pittodrie in 1946 for a bargain £1,000. He starred at juniors Muggiemoss and Hall Russell's before signing for Aberdeen in October 1938, and went back to the Granite City as trainer in 1952. Pattillo's middle-parting, bow-legged run and natural flair made him a delight to watch. He became manager of St Johnstone in January 1953.

Billy Steel, 'Mr Perpetual Motion', was born at Denny on 1 May 1923, and signed amateur forms for St Mirren in 1939, before becoming a professional with Morton during the close season of 1941. An inside forward of abundant skill, Steel's brilliant performances in 1947 for Scotland *v.* England at Wembley, and for Great Britain *v.* Rest of Europe at Hampden brought about his move to Derby County for £15,000 – a then-record fee and also the first five-figure fee paid by an English to a Scottish club.

In September 1950 this 'hard little man with bounding vitality, superb footballing brain and a stunning shot' cost Dundee £17,500 – a then-record fee for a Scottish club. 'A perfectionist who did not suffer gladly the shortcomings of less gifted colleagues', 'the Pocket Dynamo' and 'Midget Gem', was one of the greatest inside forwards of all time.

Matchday programme for the 1951/52 League Cup final against Rangers. Dundee won 3-2 through goals from Flavell, Pattillo and Boyd. The Dark Blues team was as follows: Brown, Follon, Cowan, Gallacher, Cowie, Boyd, Toner, Pattillo, Flavell, Steel, Christie.

Johnny Pattillo is congratulated by team-mates after putting Dundee 2-1 up in the 1951/52 League Cup final against Rangers at Hampden Park.

Goalkeeper Bill Brown safely gathers the ball during the 1951/52 League Cup final, with forward Willie Thornton of Rangers breathing down his neck.

Billy Steel's Scotland *v*. England international cap for the game at Wembley in 1947, which ended 1-1.

Left: Steel's Home internationals cap *v*. England, Northern Ireland and Wales in the 1948/49 season. *Right:* Steel's Scotland *v*. Wales international cap in 1951/52. Playing at Cardiff on 21 October 1951, Scotland defeated Wales 3-1.

Strike a pose. Two identical photographs of Billy Steel, except that *(left)* he wears the Morton hoops and *(right)* he models the dark blue of Dundee.

Dundee great Doug Cowie was a polished performer either in the central or left wing-half position. Born in Aberdeen on 1 May 1926, Cowie joined the Dark Blues from St Clement's Juniors in 1945, and made his debut the following year. This outstanding and inspirational half-back with an artistic approach went on to receive 20 Scotland caps. He also set a record 445 domestic appearances for the club.

Jimmy Andrews arrived at Dens Park in 1944/45 and vied for the left wing spot with George Hill and George Christie over the next seven seasons. Born at Invergordon on 1 February 1927, Andrews moved to West Ham United for £10,000 in November 1951 and, having accumulated over 100 league appearances for the 'Hammers', he later starred at Orient and QPR.

A rare programme of the 1952 Scottish Cup semi-final tie against the now defunct Third Lanark at Easter Road. Dundee won 2-0 through goals by Gerry Burrell and Billy Steel. The Dens men fielded, Henderson, Follon, Cowan, Gallacher, Cowie, Boyd, Burrell, Pattillo, Flavell, Steel and Christie.

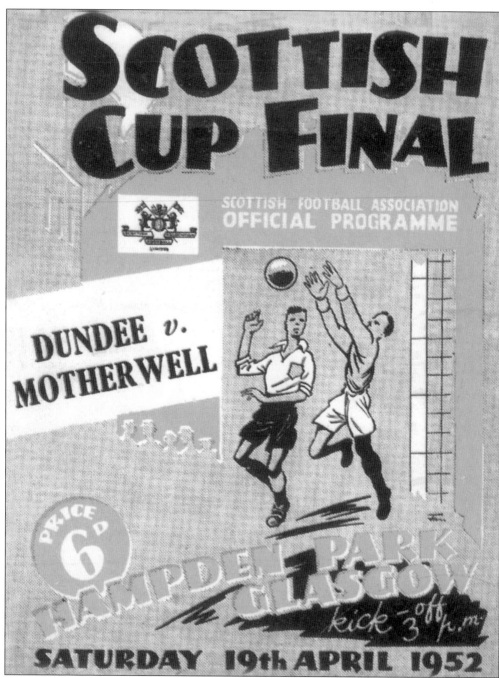

SCOTTISH CUP FINAL

SCOTTISH FOOTBALL ASSOCIATION
OFFICIAL PROGRAMME

DUNDEE v. MOTHERWELL

PRICE 6d

HAMPDEN PARK GLASGOW

kick-off 3 p.m.

SATURDAY 19th APRIL 1952

Matchday programme for the 1952 Scottish Cup final against Motherwell. Dundee's 4-0 defeat belied a close game at Hampden, which attracted a marvellous 136,274 crowd – this is second only to the 1937 final between Celtic and Aberdeen, which in itself is a club match record for Europe. The Dark Blues lined up as follows: Henderson; Follon, Cowan; Gallacher, Cowie, Boyd; Hill, Pattillo, Flavell, Steel, Christie.

Motherwell's Jimmy Watson's header hits the woodwork in the 1952 Scottish Cup Final.

In the 1952 Cup Final, Motherwell's Johnnie Aitkenhead takes a tumble and Archie Kelly appeals for a penalty. Just look at the crowd in the background! There were over 136,000 fans at this final.

Portrait of Dundee's popular and reliable half-back Doug Cowie. A League Cup winner in 1951/52 and 1952/53, he became Morton's player-coach in 1961, and had a season (1963/64) as Raith Rovers manager. A Scotland, Scottish League and 'B' internationalist, Cowie was appointed Dundee United chief scout in 1966 and held the post for many years.

Captain Alfie Boyd is chaired by team-mates after Dundee's 2-0 League Cup final win over Kilmarnock in the 1952/53 season. The team was: B. Henderson, Follon, Frew, Ziesing, Boyd, Cowie, Toner, A. Henderson, Flavell, Steel and Christie. Bobby Flavell scored the two deciding goals late in the game.

Action and excitement from the Scotland 'B' v. England 'B' game at Dens Park on 29 February 1956. An English centre forward heads past Scots pivot Danny Malloy.

Hailing from Haggs, Stirlingshire, Danny Malloy was a powerful commanding pivot who had played for Camelon Juniors before joining Dundee in 1953. He had represented the Scottish League in a 3-2 win over the Football League at Hampden Park on 16 March 1955, before being transferred to Cardiff City in December 1955 for a fee of £17,500. Malloy made over 200 league appearances for the Welshmen and ended his career at Doncaster Rovers and Clyde.

DANNY MALLOY

The Scottish 'B' team which drew 2-2 with England 'B' at Dens Park on 29 February 1956. Bill Brown is the goalkeeper, while ex-Dundee favourite Danny Malloy is pictured standing second from the right.

Custodian Bill Brown's acrobatics brought off many an 'impossible' save for Dundee in the 1950s. An Arbroath lad who came to Dens Park from Carnoustie Panmure in 1949, Bill proved himself a clever last line. He represented Scotland in the 1958 World Cup finals against France, before being transferred to Tottenham Hotspur in the summer of 1959 for £16,500. A member of Spurs' brilliant double-winning side of 1960/61, Brown had a spell with Northampton Town in 1966 and joined Toronto Falcons in April 1967.

An aerial view of Dens Park, *c.* 1970.

One of the soundest defenders in Scottish football in the 1960s, Bobby Cox arrived at Dundee from Osborne in 1956. Cool under pressure, and a master of the long pass, he often turned defence into attack with his huge clearances. A popular player, captain Cox made over 400 domestic appearances for the Dark Blues.

Dundee manager from 1954 to 1959, Willie Thornton was an Ibrox idol in the immediate post-war era. Awarded the Military Medal for valour in the field in Sicily during the Second World War, Thornton's lethal headwork and ability to snap up the half chance made him an outstanding penalty-box goal poacher. A Scottish international, Willie Thornton subsequently became manager of Partick Thistle and assistant manager of Rangers. He died in 1991, aged seventy-one.

Dundee 1956/57. From left to right, back row: Hugh Reid, Andy Irvine, Bill Brown, Ralph McKenzie, Bert Henderson, Doug Cowie. Front row: Jimmy Chalmers, Gordon Black, George Merchant, George O'Hara, George Christie.

Four

Champions and European Football (1959-1970)

Red-haired forward George McGeachie joined Dundee from Falkirk High in 1956. A maker of goals rather than a scorer of them, George was a very good reader of a game. Tricky in tight situations, he could beat a man on a sixpence. In January 1964, after a dispute with the club, he moved to Darlington for £2,000 and went on to make over 100 league appearances for that outfit.

Dundee on the defensive against Kilmarnock at Rugby Park in 1959/60. 'Keeper Pat Liney is at full stretch to try and deny Killie foward Bertie Black.

Pat Liney beats Killie's Joe McBride to the ball, as Dundee's half-back Jimmy Gabriel anxiously looks on.

Goalkeeper Liney punches clear from Dave Hilley of Third Lanark.

Dundee FC, 1960/61. From left to right, back row: Sammy Kean (trainer), B. Seith, R. Crichton, J. Duthie, P. Liney, J. Horsburgh, G. Ryden, D. Curlett, D. Cowie, A. Henderson, A. Stewart, W. Cunningham, A. Cousin, Bob Shankly (manager). Middle row: A. Gearie, G. Wallace, B. Adamson, B. McMillan, I. Ure, H. Reid, F. Jardine, B. Waddell. Front row: B. Cox, A. Hamilton, H. Robertson, A. Gilzean, G. McGeachie, A. Penman, B. Smith.

Bobby Cox (*left*) and Doug Cowie (*centre*) are watchful as striker Jim Divers attempts to score for Celtic against Dundee at Parkhead in 1960.

Alex Hamilton mops up the danger in defence at Celtic Park in 1960.

A thrilling incident at Ibrox as George Niven concedes a corner during this Rangers *v.* Dundee match in 1959/60.

Dunfermline Athletic's custodian Jim Herriot makes a fine save from an Alan Gilzean thunderbolt.

Brilliant boy prodigy and fantastic forward Andy Penman joined Dundee in January 1959 (originally as an amateur), and made his debut for the club two weeks short of his sixteenth birthday, in a match on 7 February 1959, at Hearts. Andy is the youngest-ever man to wear the dark blue of Dundee and was probably the youngest-ever amateur international. A master in precision distribution, he went to Rangers in exchange for George McLean plus £30,000 in April 1967. Capped against Holland in 1966, Andy, a diabetic, was a motor mechanic by trade. He made 278 domestic appearances for Dundee.

Hugh Robertson in the dazzling Dundee attack was a menace to many a goalkeeper. Here he is in the thick of the action against local rivals Dundee United.

Andy Penman in a tussle for the ball with Motherwell defender Thomson.

Dundee legend Alan Gilzean arrived at Dens Park in 1956 from Dundee Violet, and turned professional the following year. The Dark Blues' top domestic scorer with 154 goals, his most substantial feat was 7 against Queen of the South on 1 December 1962. Douglas Lamming described him thus: 'Subtle elegance personified, especially in the matter of the glancing header.' He scored Scotland's winner against England in 1964, and cost Spurs £72,500 that same year. Gillie had a penetrating partnership with Jimmy Greaves at White Hart Lane and played around 400 games (scoring over 100 goals) for the London club. He moved to South Africa in 1974, and managed Stevenage Town for one season (1975/76). After leaving the game he became a transport company manager in Enfield.

Dundee FC 1961/62. From left to right, back row: Davie, Liney, Wishart, Gilzean, Waddell, Seith, Smith. Front row: McGeachie, Penman, Ure, Cox, Hamilton, Cousin, Robertson.

Kilmarnock striker Joe McBride causes havoc in the Dundee goalmouth at Rugby Park.

Left: Born John Francombe Ure in Ayr on 7 December 1939, 'Ian' played for local sides Ayr Albion and Dalry Thistle before joining Dundee in 1958. A powerful centre half, Ure starred in Scotland's 2-1 win over England at Wembley in 1963 and joined Arsenal shortly afterwards for £62,500. After six seasons at Highbury he cost Manchester United £80,000 in August 1969, and ended with St Mirren during the 1973/74 season. He succeeded 'Fergie' as manager of East Stirlingshire and coached in Iceland before returning in January 1977 to take up social work in Kilmarnock. His autobiography is wittily entitled *Ure's Truly*. *Right:* Dundee's most capped player, Alex Hamilton, represented Scotland twenty-four times at full international level. 'Wee Hammie' joined the club from Westrigg Bluebell during the 1956/57 season. A classy right-back who had all-round capability and was seldom outwitted, Alex also starred for the Scottish League on eight occasions and retired in 1967. The joker of the pack, he has recently emigrated to South Africa after a spell as Dundee Violet's manager.

An afternoon to remember – Saturday 28 April 1962 – the day Dundee won the League Championship title with a 3-0 win over St Johnstone. Here, Alan Gilzean opens the scoring.

Alan Gilzean takes the acclaim of the fans after his second goal of the game.

It's all over! Dundee are the new champions of Scotland and skipper Bobby Cox celebrates the moment with the supporters.

The full squad of players celebrate winning the 1961/62 League title with this photograph taken of them in the old Muirton Park stand.

Ball-playing left half Bobby Wishart cost £3,500 from Aberdeen mid-way through the 1960/61 campaign and scored twice in his Dens debut on 7 January 1961 against arch-rivals Dundee United. Originally an inside left, Wishart moved back a position to where his expertise would prove invaluable. A key member of Dundee's 1961/62 League Championship-winning side, Bobby began his career at Merchiston Thistle. A Scottish League international, he joined Airdrieonians in August 1964.

Dundee FC 1962/63. From left to right, back row: Andy Penman, Bobby Seith, Alex Stuart, Pat Liney, Bobby Wishart, Craig Brown, Bobby Waddell. Front row: Gordon Smith, Alex Hamilton, Ian Ure, Bobby Cox, Alan Cousin, Alan Gilzean, Hugh Robertson.

The Dundee players line up for the club's first-ever competitive match in European football. The date is 5 September 1962, and the opposition I.F.C. Cologne.

Programme for the first round first leg tie against I.F.C. Cologne.

Goalkeeper Andy Penman stretches in vain to stop a German goal in the away leg of the Cologne match in 1962. He pulled on the yellow jersey during the game to replace Slater who had been injured. His spell in goal was short-lived, however, as Slater shrugged off his injury and came back on the pitch.

Alan Gilzean completes his hat-trick in Dundee's 4-1 victory over Sporting Lisbon.

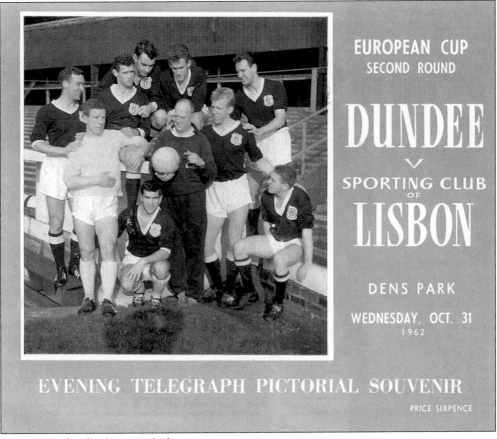

EUROPEAN CUP
SECOND ROUND

DUNDEE

v

SPORTING CLUB
OF
LISBON

DENS PARK

WEDNESDAY, OCT. 31
1962

EVENING TELEGRAPH PICTORIAL SOUVENIR

PRICE SIXPENCE

Programme for the Sporting Lisbon game.

Evening Telegraph

PICTORIAL SOUVENIR

EUROPEAN CUP — QUARTER FINALS

Dundee v Anderlecht

DENS PARK, DUNDEE

The match programme for the European Cup quarter-final tie against Anderlecht at Dens Park.

Gordon Smith (out of picture) scores the winner in the Anderlecht match.

Alan Gilzean heads the only goal of the game in the European Cup semi-final second leg against A.C. Milan. The Italians won 5-2 on aggregate and went on to win the trophy at Wembley.

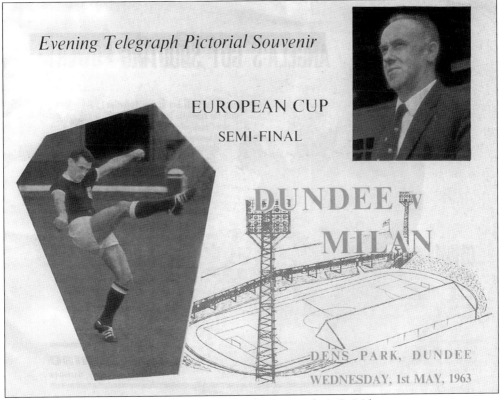

Evening Telegraph Pictorial Souvenir

EUROPEAN CUP

SEMI-FINAL

DUNDEE v MILAN

DENS PARK, DUNDEE

WEDNESDAY, 1st MAY, 1963

Match programme for the European Cup semi-final tie with A.C. Milan.

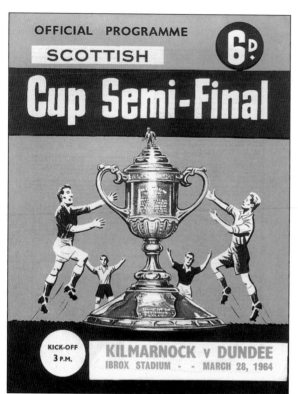

OFFICIAL PROGRAMME

6ᴰ.

SCOTTISH

Cup Semi-Final

KICK-OFF
3 P.M.

KILMARNOCK v DUNDEE
IBROX STADIUM - - MARCH 28, 1964

Dundee defeated Killie 4-0 in the 1964 Scottish Cup semi-final at Ibrox through strikes from Gilzean (2), Penman and McFadzean (o.g.).

From left to right, back row: Sammy Kean (coach), Alex Hamilton, Alan Cousin, Bert Slater, George Ryden, Alex Stuart, Bobby Seith, Bob Shankly (manager). Front row: Andy Penman, Bobby Waddell, Bobby Cox, Kenny Cameron, Alan Gilzean, Hugh Robertson.

The official match programme for the 1964 Scottish Cup final at Hampden Park. Rangers won 3-1 thanks to two very late goals in the dying seconds of the game.

Bert Slater put on a superlative goalkeeping display which thrilled the huge Hampden crowd. Here he is making a fine stop from Rangers' Ralph Brand.

A combination of Shearer and Greig clears the danger from Kenny Cameron on the Rangers goal-line.

Kenny Cameron's superb volley gives Dundee the equalising goal within a minute of Rangers' opener.

Rangers third and final goal by Ralph Brand (out of picture).

Dundee 1965/66. From left to right, back row: Ryden, Easton, Duncan, Donaldson, Law, Murray, Kinninmonth. Middle row: Swan, A. Stuart, Weir, Houston, Beattie, Cooke, Stewart. Front row: Penman, Reid, Hamilton, Harvey, Cousin, Scott, Cameron.

Autographed photos of Dark Blue favourites Andy Penman and George Stewart.

Dundee's leading scorer for three consecutive seasons (1957 to 1960), Alan Cousin packed a terrific shot in either foot. This big striker would chase paper on a windy day and always worried opponents into mistakes. He joined during the 1955/56 campaign from Alloa Y.M. and moved to Hibernian in 1965 for £15,500. He was a schoolteacher by profession, and a Scottish League and under-23 international.

New manager Bobby Ancell is welcomed to Dens Park by Alex Hamilton and Company.

Charlie Cooke, the master of wizardry, scores against his old club Aberdeen at Pittodrie in the mid-1960s.

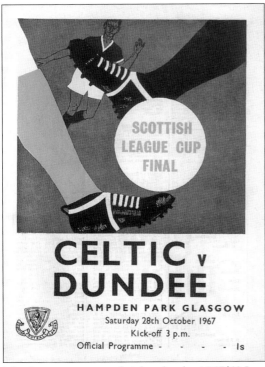

Match programme and ticket for the 1967/68 League Cup final against Celtic. Dundee pushed the 'Lisbon Lions' all the way to the wire before eventually losing 5-3. George McLean (2) and Jim McLean were the scorers.

Celt Steve Chalmers opens the scoring in the 1967/68 League Cup final.

Ex-player Scot Symon and future manager Davie White are photographed here during their Ibrox tenure in 1967.

Programme for the first leg of Dundee's Fairs Cup semi-final tie against Leeds United in 1968.

Dundee pile the pressure on the Leeds goal during the semi-final first leg at Dens which ended in a 1-1 draw. Leeds won the return game 1-0 and went on to lift the trophy.

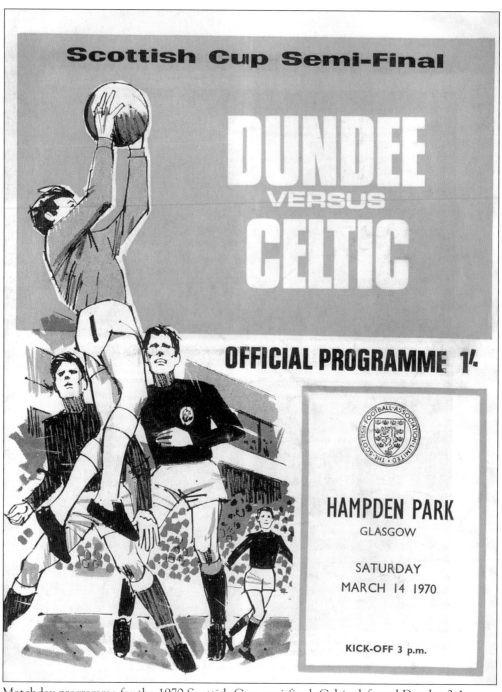

Matchday programme for the 1970 Scottish Cup semi-final. Celtic defeated Dundee 2-1.

George Stewart keeps a watchful guard on Celt Willie Wallace in the semi-final at Hampden.

Disaster! Ally Donaldson drops a Tommy Gemmell cross and Bobby Lennox pounces to win the game for Celtic with only minutes remaining.

Jocky Scott played over 400 domestic and European games for the Dark Blues and scored 154 goals (second top scorer to Alan Gilzean). Born in Aberdeen, after a brief period with Chelsea's youth team, he came to Dens in 1964. A robust and rugged forward, Jocky joined his home-town team in 1975, but returned to Tayside two years later. He has subsequently had two spells as manager of the club. Jocky Scott is an all-time Dundee great.

Originally discovered by Dundee as an amateur with Queens Park and signed from the Glasgow club in 1962 as a forward, Doug Houston showed his versatility by becoming a plucky and tenacious performer in both the left-back and left half positions. He ended his career with Rangers in 1973.

Five
League Cup Winners
(1970-1977)

A flying tackle by Dundee's Bobby Wilson stops Celtic's Harry Hood breaking through at Parkhead.

Dundee players Steve Murray and Dave Johnston.

One of the longest-serving players in Dundee's history, goalkeeper Ally Donaldson joined the club from the East Lothian junior outfit Dalkeith Thistle in 1961. He proved to be an outstanding custodian, his height being invaluable at dealing with high centres. He moved to Falkirk in 1972 for £10,000, but returned to Dens in 1976. Donaldson made around 400 appearances for the club and represented the Scottish League and Scotland at under-23 level.

Thomson Allan was a bargain free transfer from Hibernian in 1971. A brilliant last-line, Allan was confidence personified and he inspired his team-mates with immaculate handling and wonderful ability to cut out crossed balls. Capped for Scotland in 1974 against West Germany and Norway, and was a member of that year's World Cup squad. A League Cup winner, Allan ended his career with Hearts in 1980.

SCOTTISH CUP SEMI-FINAL

CELTIC v. DUNDEE

SATURDAY, APRIL 7th, 1973

KICK-OFF 3.00 p.m.

5 pence

OFFICIAL PROGRAMME

HAMPDEN
PARK

Programme for the 1973 Scottish Cup semi-final between Celtic and Dundee. The game finished goal-less.

Celt Bobby Lennox blasts the ball over the bar as George Stewart attempts to make a tackle during the 1973 Scottish Cup semi-final at Hampden.

IAN PHILLIP

DUNDEE
SCOTCARD No. 20

Defender Iain Phillip came to Dens Park from Carnoustie Panmure in 1968 as a sixteen year old, and made his first-team debut against St Mirren in September 1970. He represented the Scottish League against the Football League in March 1972 and had an outstanding game. Iain turned down Scotland boss Tommy Docherty's offer of a trip to Brazil because he had just returned from Dundee's tour of Australia and New Zealand. A strong elegant centre half, Phillip cost Crystal Palace £95,000 in 1972, but he returned to Tayside the following year. Latterly he played for Dundee United.

Prolific marksman Gordon Wallace was voted Scotland's 'Player of the Year' in 1968 whilst with Raith Rovers. He cost Dundee around £20,000 the following year. In the early 1970s, he formed a formidable twin striker partnership with John Duncan. He was Dundee's top goalscorer on three occasions and holds an honoured place in the club's history by having scored the winning goal in the 1973/74 League Cup final against Celtic.

The tag 'local lad makes good' certainly applies to the story of John Duncan. Discovered on Dundee's doorstep with Butterburn Boys' Club in 1966, the forward had a magnificent 1972/73 season for the Taysiders and finished as Scotland's leading marksman with 40 goals. He also netted both the Scottish League goals in a 2-2 draw with the Football League at Hampden on 27 March 1973; surprisingly, he never gained a full cap. Duncan cost Spurs £140,000 in October 1974 and he later moved to Derby County for £170,000. He subsequently became manager at Scunthorpe, Chesterfield and Ipswich Town.

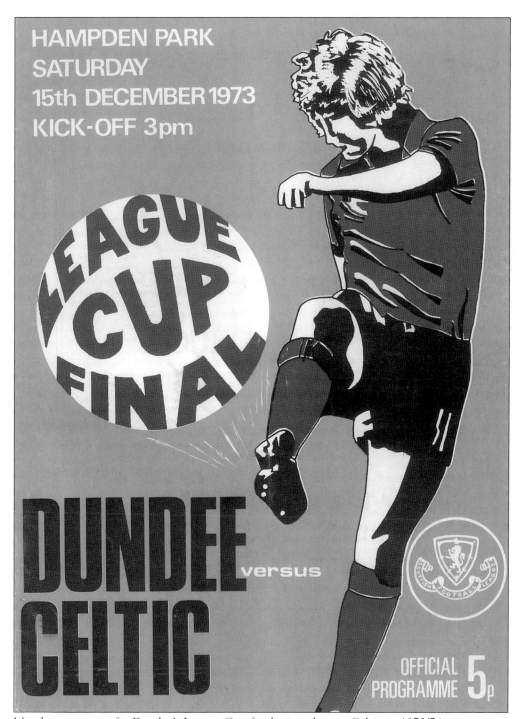

HAMPDEN PARK
SATURDAY
15th DECEMBER 1973
KICK-OFF 3pm

LEAGUE CUP FINAL

DUNDEE versus CELTIC

OFFICIAL PROGRAMME 5p

Match programme for Dundee's League Cup final triumph over Celtic in 1973/74 season.

A fine catch by Thomson Allan on a rainswept Hampden Park in the League Cup final against Celtic.

Allan comes to Dundee's rescue again, this time to foil Kenny Dalglish.

The goal which sealed the Dark Blues' League Cup final success over Celtic. Gordon Wallace's drive gives goalkeeper Ally Hunter no chance.

Thomson Allan jumps for a high ball with Celtic skipper Billy McNeill.

A sight for sore eyes – captain Tommy Gemmell raises the League Cup above his head to the acclaim of the supporters.

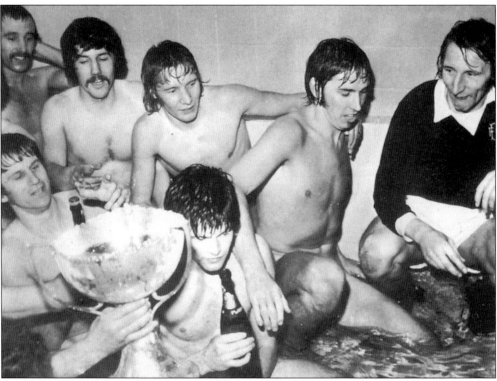

The Dark Blue heroes celebrate with champagne in the bath.

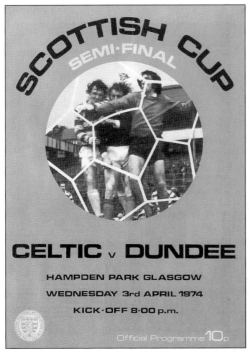
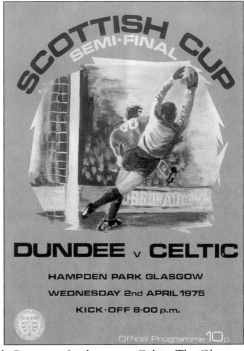

Programmes for Dundee's 1974 and 1975 Scottish Cup semi-finals against Celtic. The Glasgow club won both games by a solitary goal to nil.

Custodian Thomson Allan punches the ball clear of Celtic forward Dixie Deans at Dens Park in the 1974/75 season.

Striker Bobby Hutcheson scores for Dundee against Rangers at Dens Park in 1974/75 season.

Above left: Bobby 'Trigger' Robinson was a consistent performer in midfield for Dundee in the 1970s. Capped on four occasions by Scotland, he joined the Dark Blues in 1972 from Falkirk. A player with plenty of speed and poise, he starred at Dundee United, Hearts and Raith Rovers in the later stages of his career. He died at home in Forfar in December 1996, aged just forty-six. *Above right* and *below left* and *right*: Dundee defenders of the 1970s, Tommy Gemmell Bobby Wilson and Alex Caldwell.

Above left: Programme for the 1977 Scottish Cup semi-final, which Celtic won 2-0. *Above right:* Dundee goalscoring great Billy Pirri hit a remarkable 44 goals in 1976/77 and 38 the following season. *Below left:* Wilson Hoggan. *Below right:* Bobby Ford.